NEW YORK IS...

NEW YORK IS...

The Metropolitan Museum of Art

New York

NEW YORK CITY is a place of possibility. From people to experiences, from cultures to religions, from politics to economics, the possibilities are endless. These endless possibilities make New York the most diverse city in the world, a city that cannot be described in a single word.

In fact, this book uses nearly two hundred words to describe the global metropolis on the Hudson River. Illustrated with works of art from The Metropolitan Museum of Art's collection, the words in the following pages are concise reflections on Gotham. New York is shape, New York is line. New York is finance, New York is industry. New York is bustling, New York is deserted. Some of the words speak to observations and experiences, while others reference the accompanying work of art.

All of the selected works of art reach across the Museum's collection from paintings and costumes to sculpture and contemporary photographs. Detailed commentary about the works can be found on the Museum's website at www.metmuseum.org.

Because anything is possible in Gotham, readers are encouraged to observe and to create their own descriptions of New York.

New York is shape,

New York is line.

New York is iconic,

Statue of Liberty (detail)
Published by J. Koehler, New York and Berlin, early 20th century
Color lithograph, $5\,^1/_2 \times 3\,^1/_2$ in.
The Jefferson R. Burdick Collection, Gift of Jefferson R. Burdick, Burdick 455, p. 11v(5)

New York is unfamiliar.

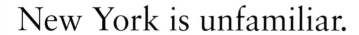

New York is dynamic,

New York is static.

New York is illustration,

AUTOBIOGRAPHICAL POEM by PINERO · ATTORNEY STREET HANDBALL COURT 1982

I WAS BORN IN A BARREL of BUTCHER KNIVES· RAISED BETWEEN TWO 45's· ON A SATURDAY N
AND THE HUSTLER WERE STALKING THEIR PREY· WHERE THE CODE WAS CRIME IN NEON LIGHTS AND THE WEA
PROWL WITH A TIGERS GROWL IN SEARCH of THEIR LETHAL BLOW· WHERE CRIME BEGIN WHEN DAUGHTER FO
THE SAKE of BREAD· WHERE EVEN GOD WAS CORRUPT· AND FEW GO DOWN CRYING AS GO DOWN TRYING C
YEA IT SEEM I WAS A MORED DREAM I KNEW THE SLEIGHT of HAND of A MURPHY MAN I COULD TAKE A SAILOR POKE WITH
OUT LIGHTNING· DROWNED A DROP of WATER· · BUT HANDCUFF ON THE WIND LOCK THUNDER N JAIL · · SLAPPED·

ITS THE REAL DEAL NEAL
I'M GOING TO ROCK YOUR WORLD
MAKE YOUR PLANETS TWIRL
AIN'T NO WACK ATTACK

New York is graffiti.

Attorney Street (Handball Court with Autobiographical Poem by Piñero)

Martin Wong, American, 1946–1999

Oil on canvas, 35¹/₂ × 48 in., 1982–84

Edith C. Blum Fund, 1984 1984.110

New York is industry,

New York is finance.

New York is a walk in the park,

New York is a day at the beach.

New York is spectacle,

New York is commonplace.

Seventh Avenue and 16th Street, New York (detail)
Mark Baum, American, 1903–1997
Oil on canvas, 30 × 28 in., 1932
Edith C. Blum Fund, 1983 1983.122.2

LA FESTA 'E TUTT' 'E FESTE
11ma GRANDIOSA FESTA DI

S. GENNARO

15-16-17-18-19 SETTEMBRE, 1948

Diretta FERRUCCIO BURCO

GRANDE RIFFA

EXTRA PREMIO

PIZZERIA
RESTAURANT
118

New York is light,

Mulberry Street

Sid Grossman, American, 1913–1955

Gelatin silver print, 13¹/₄ × 10⁷/₁₆ in., 1948

Purchase, The Horace W. Goldsmith Foundation Gift,

through Joyce and Robert Menschel, 1990 1990.1139.2

© Estate of Sid Grossman,

courtesy Howard Greenberg Gallery, New York

New York is shadow.

New York is shared spaces,

New York is secret gardens.

Backyards, Brooklyn
Ogden M. Pleissner, American, 1905–1983
Oil on canvas, 24 × 30⅛ in., 1932
Arthur Hoppock Hearn Fund, 1932 32.80.2

New York is glamour,

New York is grit.

New York is organized,

The City of New York: Longworth's Explanatory Map and Plan (detail)

James DeForest Stout, American, 1783–1868

Printed by Daniel Fanshawe, American, 19th century

Hand-colored engraving, 19¹/₈ × 19¹/₈ in., 1817

The Edward W. C. Arnold Collection of New York Prints, Maps, and Pictures,

Bequest of Edward W. C. Arnold, 1954 54.90.630

New York is chaos.

New York is overhead,

New York is underfoot.

New York is art,

New York is architecture.

New York is water,

New York is steel.

New York is lively,

New York is idyllic.

Spring in Central Park
Adolf Dehn, American, 1895–1968
Watercolor on paper, 17⁷/₈ × 27¹/₄ in., 1941
Fletcher Fund, 1941 41.113ab

adolf Dehn.

New York is gilded,

New York is unadorned.

New York is ambition,

New York is chance.

Matlin 32

New York is drawn,

New York is painted.

Union Square, Looking up Park Avenue
Fairfield Porter, American, 1907–1975
Oil on canvas, 62¼ × 72 in., 1975
Gift of Mrs. Fairfield Porter, 1978   1978.224

New York is community,

New York is solitude.

New York is glistening,

Night Scene from the Pierre Hotel—Showing Three Bridges
Peter Fink, American, 1907–1984
Gelatin silver print, 13⅝ × 16¹³/₁₆ in., 1960s
Purchase, Cournand Foundation Inc. Gift, 1965 65.681.13
© Estate of Peter Fink / Artists Rights Society (ARS), New York

New York is subdued.

New York is fleeting,

Central Park, Winter
William James Glackens, American, 1870–1938
Oil on canvas, 25 × 30 in., ca. 1905
George A. Hearn Fund, 1921 21.164

New York is enduring.

Trinity Church, New York

Edward J. Steichen, American (b. Luxembourg), 1879–1973

Gum bichromate over platinum print, 19 x 14³/₄ in., 1904, printed later

Alfred Stieglitz Collection, 1933 33.43.41

New York is on stage,

Design for Lyceum Theatre, New York
Louis Comfort Tiffany, American, 1848–1933
Watercolor, pen and gold-colored bronze metallic ink, brown and black India
ink, and graphite on tan-colored wove paper; 11⁷/₁₆ × 10¹⁵/₁₆ in., ca. 1885
The Elisha Whittelsey Collection, The Elisha Whittelsey Fund, 1953 53.679.1824

New York is on film.

Still from an Untitled Film
Cindy Sherman, American, b. 1954
Gelatin silver print, 7⅛ x 9⁷/₁₆ in., 1978
Purchase, The Horace W. Goldsmith Foundation Gift,
through Joyce and Robert Menschel, 1992 1992.5147
© Cindy Sherman

THE EMPIRE CITY,
Birdseye view of NEW-YORK and Environs.

New York is distinctive,

New York is repetition.

New York is the sea,

New York is the sky.

Fourteenth Street, High Noon

John Button, American, 1929–1982

Gouache on paper, 14¹/₈ × 20 in., 1977

Gift of Dr. and Mrs. Robert E. Carroll, 1979 1979.138.1

© Estate of John Button, courtesy of ClampArt, NYC

New York is inspiring,

New York is exhausting.

New York is joyous,

New York is sensational.

New York is famous,

New York is anonymous.

New York is fashion,

New York is design.

New York is expansive,

New York from the Steeple of St. Paul's Church, Looking East, South, and West (detail)

Henry A. Papprill, British, 1817–1896

After John William Hill, American (b. England), 1812–1879

Published by Henry J. Megarey, American, 1818–1845

Color aquatint and etching; second state of three, 21 1/4 × 36 3/16 in., 1849

The Edward W. C. Arnold Collection of New York Prints, Maps, and Pictures,

Bequest of Edward W. C. Arnold, 1954 54.90.587

New York is confining.

New York is sewn,

Ensemble, detail of a jacket
American (probably), ca. 1935
Multicolor printed rayon crêpe, L. 29¼ in.
The Jacqueline Loewe Fowler Costume Collection,
Gift of Jacqueline Loewe Fowler, 1996 1996.135.2a–c

New York is quilted.

New York is descriptive,

New York is advertising.

New York is dazzling,

New York is stormy.

New York is food,

Tables for Ladies
Edward Hopper, American, 1882–1967
Oil on canvas, 48¹/₄ × 60¹/₄ in., 1930
George A. Hearn Fund, 1931 31.62

New York is culture.

The Lafayette
John Sloan, American, 1871–1951
Oil on canvas, 30¹/₂ × 36¹/₈ in., 1927
Gift of The Friends of John Sloan, 1928 28.18

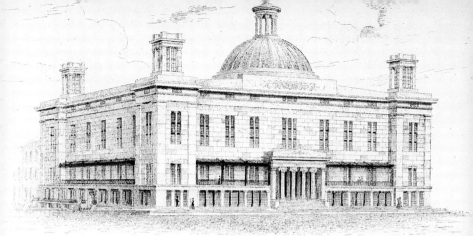

DESIGN MADE FOR ASTOR'S HOTEL
BY I. TOWN & A. J. DAVIS, ARC'TS.

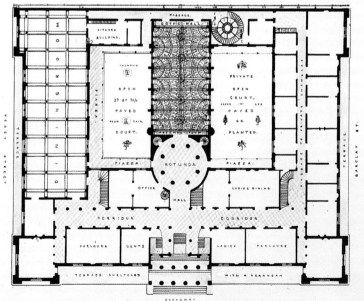

PLAN BY ITHIEL TOWN, ARC'T.
FOR ASTOR'S HOTEL.
NEW-YORK. 1832.

New York is planned,

New York is happenstance.

New York is celebration,

New York is remembrance.

Untitled, New York, 1998

Mitch Epstein, American, b. 1952

Chromogenic print, 22 1/2 × 27 3/4 in., 1998

Gift of The Peter T. Joseph Foundation, 2002 2002.376.7

© Mitch Epstein / Black River Productions, Ltd.

New York is music,

New York is poetry.

EPITAPH

THEODORE   DREISER

New York is adventure,

Icarus, Empire State Building
Lewis Hine, American, 1874–1940
Gelatin silver print, 7³/₈ × 9⁵/₁₆ in., 1930
Ford Motor Company Collection, Gift of Ford
Motor Company and John C. Waddell, 1987 1987.1100.119

New York is routine.

New York is ephemera,

Statue of Liberty, Bedloe's Island, New York
Published by J. Koehler, New York and Berlin, early 20th century
Color lithograph, pierced and layered; $3^1/_2 \times 5^1/_2$ in., ca. 1905
The Jefferson R. Burdick Collection, Gift of Jefferson R. Burdick, Burdick 455, p. 9r(4)

d, NEW YORK Harbor

New York is sculpture.

New York is angled,

New York is curved.

New York is Victorian,

New York is Art Deco.

The Gift and Art Shop
Donald Deskey, American, 1894–1989
Printed by Geyer Publications, Andrew Geyer Inc. Publishers
Printed paper, 11 × 8 in., 1928
Anonymous Gift, 1999 1999.432

New York is love,

Couple at Coney Island, New York

Walker Evans, American, 1903–1975

Gelatin silver print, 8 × 5¹³/₁₆ in., 1928

Ford Motor Company Collection, Gift of Ford Motor Company and John C. Waddell, 1987 1987.1100.110

© Walker Evans Archive, The Metropolitan Museum of Art

New York is heartbreak.

New York is expressive,

New York is mundane.

New York is edifice,

Metropolitan Life Insurance Building, New York

Published by Detroit Publishing Company, American, 1908–09

Color lithograph, 5 ¹/₂ × 3 ¹/₂ in.

The Jefferson R. Burdick Collection, Gift of Jefferson R. Burdick, Burdick 416, p. 51v(3)

12740 METROPOLITAN LIFE INSURANCE BUILDING, NEW YORK.

New York is frame.

From My Window at An American Place, Southwest
Alfred Stieglitz, American, 1864–1946
Gelatin silver print, $7^9/_{16}$ × $9^1/_2$ in., 1932
Alfred Stieglitz Collection, 1949 49.55.48

New York is festive,

New York is dreary.

Rainy Day at Madison Square, New York City
American, 1900s–1930s
Photomechanical reproduction, 3^9/$_{16}$ × 5^1/$_2$ in.
Walker Evans Archive, 1994 1994.264.107.575

New York is built,

Empire State Building
Lewis Hine, American, 1874–1940
Gelatin silver print, 3¹⁵/₁₆ × 4¹³/₁₆ in., 1930s
Ford Motor Company Collection, Gift of Ford Motor
Company and John C. Waddell, 1987 1987.1100.325

New York is natural.

New York is song,

New York is dance.

Curve at Brooklyn Terminal, Brooklyn Bridge, New York

New York is trains,

Curve at Brooklyn Terminal, Brooklyn Bridge, New York (detail)
Published by George P. Hall & Son, American, active 1886–1914
Photomechanical reproduction, $5^{1}/_{2} \times 3^{9}/_{16}$ in., ca. 1910
Walker Evans Archive, 1994 1994.264.38.2

New York is automobiles.

The Old New York Post Office
Junius Allen, American, 1898–1962
Oil on canvas, mounted on Masonite, 36 × 42 in., 1939–40
George A. Hearn Fund, 1940 40.85

New York is stone,

New York is glass.

New York is a moment,

Financial District, from the Hotel Bossert
Samuel H. Gottscho, American, 1875–1971
Gelatin silver print, 6⁹/₁₆ × 9⁷/₁₆ in., 1933, printed later
Purchase, Florance Waterbury Bequest, 1970 1970.660.11

New York is an impression.

Winter in Union Square (detail)

Childe Hassam, American, 1859–1935

Oil on canvas, 18¹/₄ × 18 in., 1889–90

Gift of Ethelyn McKinney, in memory of her brother, Glenn Ford McKinney, 1943 43.116.2

New York is bustling,

Pennsylvania Station (detail)

Arnold Eagle, American (b. Hungary), 1909–1992

Gelatin silver print, 13 $\frac{1}{8}$ x 10 $\frac{3}{16}$ in., 1941

Gift of the artist, 1990 1990.1116.1

New York is deserted.

New York is law,

New Court House.

New York.

New York is order.

New Court House, New York
American, 1900–1930s
Photomechanical reproduction, $3^{9}/_{16}$ × $5^{1}/_{2}$ in.
Walker Evans Archive, 1994 1994.264.33.38

New York is daring,

5464   YARD OF A TENEMENT, NEW YORK.

New York is banal.

Yard of a Tenement, New York
Detroit Publishing Company, American, early 20th century
Color lithograph, $3^{1}/_{2} \times 5^{1}/_{2}$ in.
The Jefferson R. Burdick Collection, Gift of Jefferson R. Burdick, Burdick 416, p. 21v(3)

New York is streetscape,

The Photographer

Jacob Lawrence, American, 1917–2000

Watercolor, gouache, and pencil on paper, 22⅛ × 30½ in., 1942

Purchase, Lila Acheson Wallace Gift, 2001 2001.205

© The Jacob and Gwendolyn Lawrence Foundation, Seattle / Artists Rights Society (ARS), New York

New York is landscape.

New York is observation,

New York is perspective.

New York is posh,

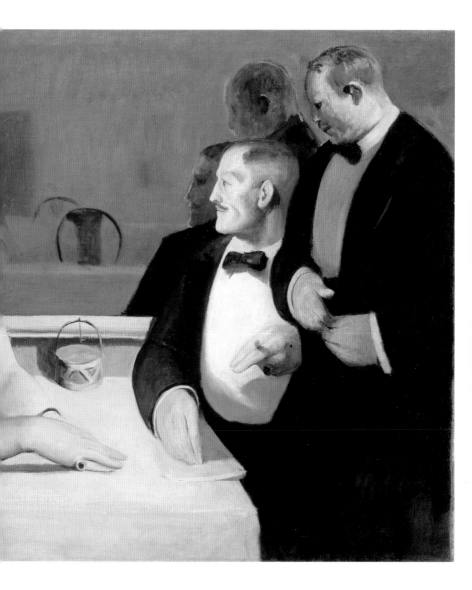

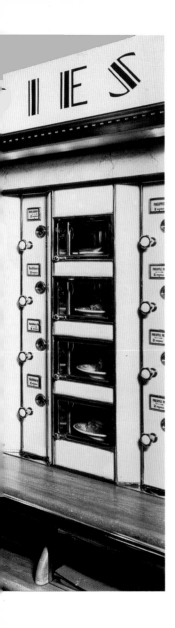

New York is spare.

NEW YORK CITY W.P.A. ART PROJECT

"Playground"

G- 9509

Ruth Chaney

11

$+$ New York is play,

Playground
Ruth Chaney, American, b. 1908
Published by the Works Progress Administration
Serigraph, 13 × 9¼ in., 1935–43
Gift of the Works Progress Administration, New York, 1943 43.33.832

New York is study.

"*Babylon*"

New York is drafted,

New York is acted.

"Lullaby of Broadway" from Gold Diggers of 1935

American, 1935

Gelatin silver print, 7 1/2 × 9 5/8 in.

Ford Motor Company Collection, Gift of Ford Motor Company

and John C. Waddell, 1987 1987.1100.142

GD- 16

New York is a voyage,

New York is a jaunt.

New York is real,

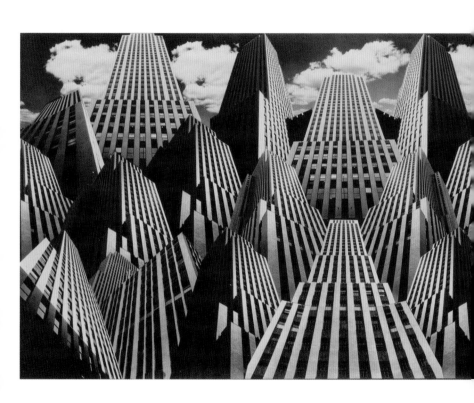

New York is illusion.

Skyscrapers

Thurman Rotan, American, 1903–1991

Gelatin silver print, 8³/₁₆ × 16¹/₁₆ in., 1932

Ford Motor Company Collection, Gift of Ford Motor Company

and John C. Waddell, 1987 1987.1100.280

New York is energetic,

Queensboro Bridge at Night

Joseph W. Golinkin, American, 1896–1977

Published by American Artists Group

Commercial photomechanical process, 6 × 4 1/4 in.

The Jefferson R. Burdick Collection, Gift of Jefferson R. Burdick, Burdick 574, p. 87

New York is tranquil.

The Bronx River

Ernest Lawson, American, 1873–1939

Oil on canvas, 21 × 25 in., ca. 1910

Gift of Mrs. J. Augustus Barnard, 1979 1979.490.13

LUNA PARK

Y ISLAND.

New York is amusement,

Luna Park, Coney Island
American, early 20th century
Photomechanical reproduction, 3⁹/₁₆ × 5¹/₂ in.
Walker Evans Archive, 1994 1994.264.37.34

New York is exertion.

Steamfitter

Lewis Hine, American, 1874–1940

Gelatin silver print, 13⁹/₁₆ × 9¹/₄, 1910s

Gift of Clarence McK. Lewis, 1954 54.549.56

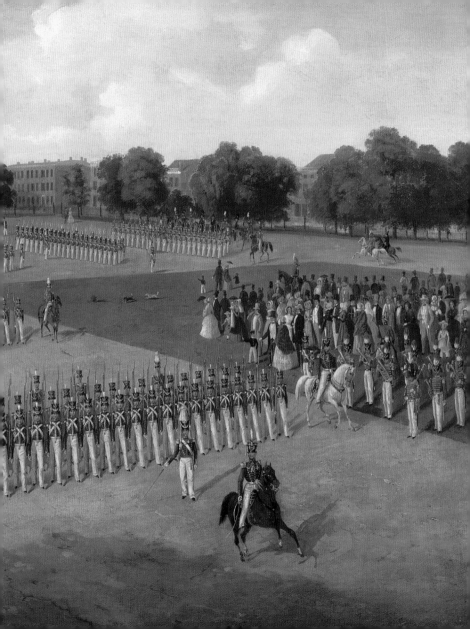

New York is history,

New York is vision.

New York is evocative,

New York is reflection.

New York is performance,

The Cathedrals of Broadway
Florine Stettheimer, American, 1871–1944
Oil on canvas, 60⅛ × 50⅛ in., 1929
Gift of Ettie Stettheimer, 1953 53.24.3

New York is sport.

New York is symmetry,

New York is juxtaposition.

South Street Bridge

Dong Kingman, American, 1911–2000

Watercolor on paper, 21¹/₂ × 29³/₄ in., 1955

George A. Hearn Fund, 1955 55.101

New York is monumental,

New York is ordinary.

Daily News

Dona Nelson, American, b. 1952

Oil on canvas, 84 × 60 in., 1983

Purchase, Emma P. Ziprik Memorial Fund Gift,

in memory of Fred and Emma P. Ziprik, 1984 1984.266

DAILY NEWS

NUCLEAR ARMS BUILDUP

DAILY NEWS

Isis breeze, 5-0
Roll Rangers, 2-0

New York is by foot,

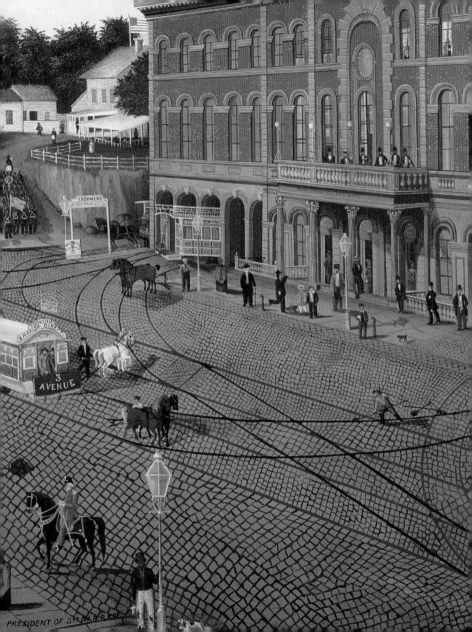

New York is by hoof.

New York is green space,

New York is pavement.

New York is angelic,

New York is trouble.

New York is brownstone,

NOVELTY IRON WORKS, FOOT OF 12.ᵗʰ S

Steam Boilers, Iron Ships and Boats, Sugar Mills, Wrought Iron Sugar Kettles.
Improved Steam Clarifiers and Evaporators Vacuum Pans, Hydraulic

STILLMAN, ALLEN & Cᵒ.
Iron Founders Steam Engine and General Machinery Manufacturer

New York is iron.

Novelty Iron Works, Foot of 12th St. E. R. New York.
Stillman, Allen & Co., Iron Founders,
Steam Engine and General Machinery Manufacturers
John Penniman, American, 1817–1850
Lithographed by G. & W. Endicott, New York
Color lithograph with hand coloring, 18¹⁵/₁₆ × 31¼ in., 1841–44
The Edward W. C. Arnold Collection of New York Prints, Maps, and Pictures,
Bequest of Edward W. C. Arnold, 1954 54.90.588

New York is grand,

Grand Central Terminal, New York, Main Concourse (detail)

Published by Detroit Publishing Company, American, early 20th century

Color lithograph, $3^{1}/_{2} \times 5^{1}/_{2}$ in.

The Jefferson R. Burdick Collection, Gift of Jefferson R. Burdick, Burdick 417, p. 6r(4)

New York is conventional.

View from the Artist's Window, Grove Street
Robert Frederick Blum, American, 1857–1903
Oil on canvas, 22$^5/_{16}$ × 19$^1/_2$ in., ca. 1900
Gift of Margaret and Raymond J. Horowitz, 1976 1976.340.2

New York is religion,

St. Patrick's Cathedral, New York

Published by Detroit Publishing Company, American, early 20th century

Color lithograph, $5^1/_2 \times 3^1/_2$ in.

The Jefferson R. Burdick Collection, Gift of Jefferson R. Burdick, Burdick 416, p. 25v(5)

6891. ST. PATRICK'S CATHEDRAL, NEW YORK. COPYRIGHT, 1903, BY DETROIT PHOTOGRAPHIC CO.

New York is commerce.

New York is cityscape,

New York is seascape.

New York is tradition,

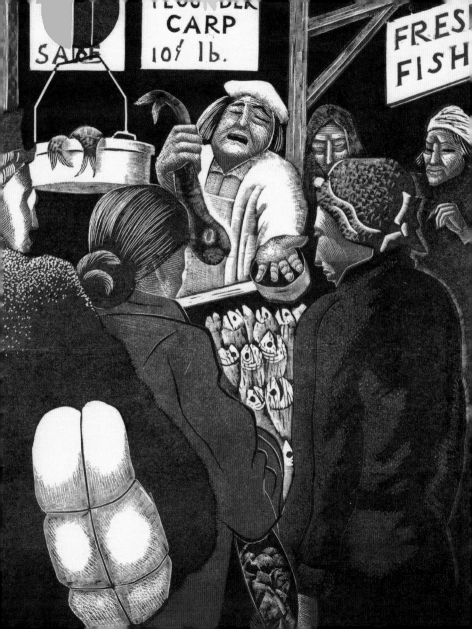

New York is invention.

New York is authentic,

New York is atmospheric.

New York is sketched,

New York is photographed.

[Walker Evans in Central Park Zoo, New York City]
American, 1947
Gelatin silver print, $2^3/_4 \times 1^{15}/_{16}$ in.
Anonymous Gift, 1999 1999.246.75

New York is fantasy,

Something's Got to Give
Barney Tobey, American, 1906–1989
Published by Fantasia (American Artists Group)
Commercial color process, 4 x 7 ¹/₂ in., 1957
The Jefferson R. Burdick Collection, Gift of Jefferson R. Burdick, Burdick 565, p. 40r(1)

New York is mythology.

New York is outside a window,

New York is on a street.

New York is vibrant,

Lower Manhattan from the River, Number 1
John Marin, American, 1870–1953
Watercolor, charcoal, and graphite on paper, 21⁷/₈ × 26¹/₂ in., 1921
Alfred Stieglitz Collection, 1949 49.70.122
© Estate of John Marin / Artists Rights Society (ARS), New York

New York is bleak.

New York is politics,

Encore

New York is theater.

New York is before,

New York is after.

VIGNETTES OF MANHATTAN

BY

BRANDER MATTHEWS

ILLUSTRATED

HARPER & BROTHERS PUBLISHERS

New York is literary,

Vignettes of Manhattan by Brander Matthews
Edward Penfield, American, 1866–1925
Published by Harper & Brothers Publishers
Commercial lithograph; yellow, vermillion, and blue, 12¹³/₁₆ × 9³/₈ in.
Gift of Bessie Potter Vonnoh, 1941 41.12.49

New York is gossip.

New York is a game,

Pool Parlor

Jacob Lawrence, American, 1917–2000

Watercolor and gouache on paper, 31 1/8 × 22 7/8 in., 1942

Arthur Hoppock Hearn Fund, 1942 42.167

© The Jacob and Gwendolyn Lawrence Foundation, Seattle / Artists Rights Society (ARS), New York

New York is a party.

Robert Frank

New York is a stoop,

New York is a fire escape.

New York is abstract,

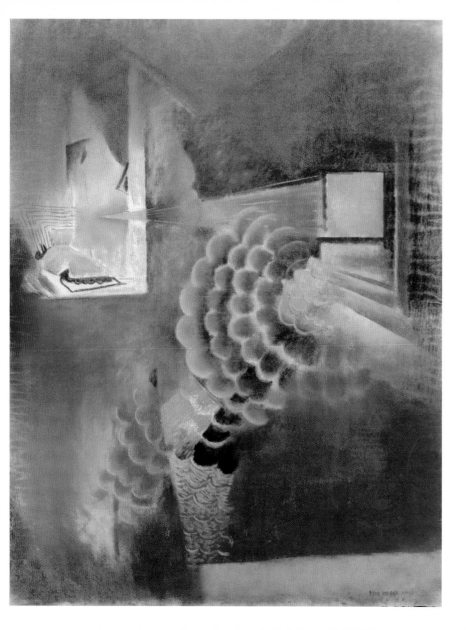

New York is pastiche.

72270 EMPIRE STATE BUILDING, NEW YORK. COPYRIGHT AMEMYA.

New York is day,

Empire State Building

Published by Detroit Publishing Company, American, early 20th century

Color lithograph, $5 \frac{1}{2} \times 3 \frac{1}{2}$ in.

The Jefferson R. Burdick Collection, Gift of Jefferson R. Burdick, Burdick 417 p.12r(2)

New York is night.

72260 EMPIRE STATE BUILDING, NEW YORK, N. Y.

New York is opulent,

New York is humble.

New York is columns,

New York is arches.

New York is active,

New York is idle.

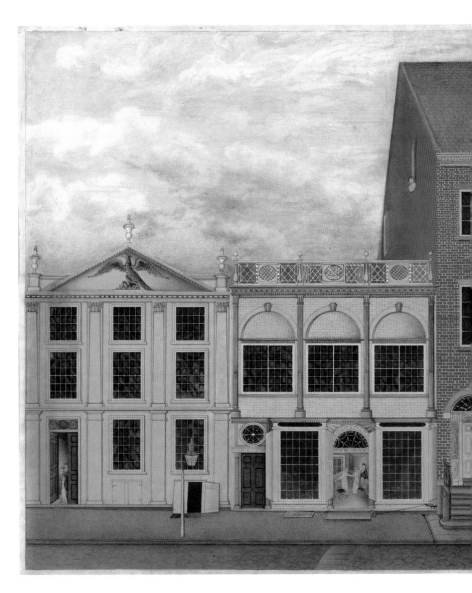

New York is trade,

The Shop and Warehouse of Duncan Phyfe, 168–172 Fulton Street, New York City
Formerly attributed to John Rubens Smith, American, 1775–1849
Watercolor, black ink, and gouache on white laid paper, 15⅞ × 19⅝ in., ca. 1816
Rogers Fund, 1922 22.28.1

New York is transportation.

New York is printed,

New York is etched.

New York is constructed,

New York is demolished.

Demolished Building, New York
Herbert Randall, American, b. 1936
Gelatin silver print, 13$^7/_{16}$ × 9$^1/_4$ in., 1963
David Hunter McAlpin Fund, 1966 66.642.1

New York is movement,

The Green Car

William James Glackens, American, 1870–1938

Oil on canvas, 24 × 32 in., 1910

Arthur Hoppock Hearn Fund, 1937 37.73

New York is still.

Sutton Place, New York City
Jan Staller, American, b. 1952
Chromogenic print, 6¹/₄ × 6³/₁₆ in., 1983
Gift of the artist, 1984 1984.1018

New York is the past,

New York is the future.

Future New York, "The City of Skyscrapers"
American, early 20th century
Photomechanical reproduction, 5 1/2 × 3 9/16 in.
Walker Evans Archive, 1994 1994.264.20.2

Published by The Metropolitan Museum of Art

The Metropolitan Museum of Art
1000 Fifth Avenue
New York, NY 10028
www.metmuseum.org

Produced by the Department of Printed Product, The Metropolitan Museum of Art: Text by Mimi Tribble; design by Seoyeon Sally Lee; photography by The Metropolitan Museum of Art Photograph Studio.

Printed in Hong Kong
17 16 15   10 9 8 7 6 5 4 3 2

ISBN: 978-1-58839-448-4